# SMOOTHIES FOR KIDS

## CHARLOTTE GIBBS

# TABLE OF CONTENTS

## CHAPTER 1

### FRUITYLICIOUS SMOOTHIES

## BONUS: LET'S ADD YOGURT!

## CHAPTER 2

### VEGGIE SMOOTHIES     77

# CHAPTER 3

## SUPER SMOOTHIE BOWLS!

# CHAPTER 4

## BONUS RECIPES! LET'S GET CREATIVE

# WELCOME TO YOUR SMOOTHIE ADVENTURE!

Hey there! Are you ready to go on a yummy adventure? Well, get your blenders ready (with your parent's supervision, of course!), and let's dive into the colorful, yummy world of smoothies!

Smoothies are like magic potions made from fruits, veggies, and all kinds of tasty ingredients. They taste amazing, right? But the extra awesome thing is that they also give you lots of energy to play, run, and have fun all day long! Plus, they are packed with vitamins and good stuff that help you grow big and strong. It also means when you want a sweet, delicious snack, your mom and dad will be happy to let you have as much as you like because they know how good they are for you.

Making smoothies is super easy, and a lot of fun too. All you need are some fresh ingredients, a blender, and your imagination. You can mix and match different fruits, veggies, and other fun ingredients to find the perfect smoothies for you.

Are you excited? Let's get blending and make some tasty, colorful, and healthy treats! Remember, the best part of making smoothies is having fun and getting creative.

**READY
SET!
SMOOTHIE!**

# TOOLS AND GADGETS FOR BLENDING FUN!

Before we start blending up some tasty smoothies, let's gather all the things you'll need. Don't worry—it's easy!

Tools to Have in Your Kitchen:

## ✓ BLENDER

The MVP of smoothie-making! A blender is like a magic whirlpool that mixes all the ingredients into a delicious drink. Blenders can be powerful, so always ask an adult for help when turning it on and off.

## ✓ MEASURING CUPS AND SPOONS

These are the secret code breakers of the kitchen—they help us measure just the right amount of ingredients so our smoothies taste perfect every time.

## ✓ CUTTING BOARD AND KID-SAFE KNIFE

You'll need these to chop up fruits and veggies. If you're using a regular knife, always ask an adult for help. There are also kid-safe knives that work well for softer fruits like bananas and strawberries!

**Quick reminder: safety first!**

Always ask for help from an adult when using kitchen tools.

## ✓ SPATULA OR SPOON

This is for scooping out every last drop of your smoothie from the blender. We don't want to waste any deliciousness!

### ✓ Glasses, Cups and Bowls

You'll need something to pour your smoothie into! Choose a fun cup, or if you're making a smoothie bowl, grab a bowl and get ready to add some yummy toppings.

### ✓ Reusable Straws or Spoons

Reusable straws or spoons make drinking or slurping your smoothie extra fun. Plus, they're better for the planet!

### ✓ Freezer and Ice Cube Trays

Smoothies are best when they're cold! Sometimes we add ice cubes or even freeze some fruits ahead of time to make your smoothie extra chilly and thick.

There will be recipes in this book where you will need other tools and equipment, but don't you worry! Everything is specified in each recipe.

Now that you've gathered all the necessary basic tools, let's get blending!

# MEASURING MAGIC

Getting the right amount of ingredients can make your smoothies even tastier! Here's a simple guide to help you scoop, pour and, blend like a pro.

Measuring Cups and Spoons

- **1 Cup**: The biggest scoop! This is great for things like milk or fruits.
- **½ Cup**: Half the size of the big scoop! Use it when you need a little less of something.
- **¼ Cup**: A small scoop for when you just need a little bit.
- **Tablespoon (Tbsp)**: Like a mini scoop! Perfect for things like honey or nut butter.
- **Teaspoon (tsp)**: Even smaller, great for spices or a pinch of vanilla.

If you don't have measuring cups, no worries! You can use a kitchen scale to weigh the ingredients. Here's a handy chart with measurements in cups and their equivalents in ounces, milliliters, pounds, and grams.

| Cups | Ounces (oz) | Milliliters (ml) | Pounds (lb) | Grams (g) |
|---|---|---|---|---|
| 1 Cup | 8 oz | 240 ml | 0.5 lb | 113.4 g |
| ½ Cup | 4 oz | 120 ml | 0.25 lb | 56.7 g |
| ¼ Cup | 2 oz | 60 ml | 0.125 lb | 28.3 g |
| Tablespoon (Tbsp) | 0.5 oz | 15 ml | - | 14.2 g |
| Teaspoon (tsp) | 0.17 oz | 5 ml | - | 4.2 g |

**SMOOTHIE TIP!**

I know this can be confusing, so make sure to ask your parents for guidance when using a scale and measuring ingredients! Remember, a little extra fruit never hurt anyone!

# SWEETENERS FROM NATURE

It's pretty cool that our smoothies are super yummy and don't have added sugar! But if you want to make them a little sweeter, here are some healthy options you can add:

## Our Sweet Picks:

**Organic Honey:** This sweet stuff comes from bees and is really tasty! Just a teaspoon or two is enough to make your smoothie sweet. Plus, it can help when you have a sore throat!

**Pure Maple Syrup:** This syrup comes from trees and seriously makes your smoothies taste like candy! Make sure to use the good stuff that's organic, not the kind for pancakes. It gives you a nice energy boost, too!

**Dates:** These sweet, chewy fruits are like nature's candy! You can blend a couple of them into your smoothie for a yummy, sugary flavor, plus they have fiber and nutrients which are great for you.

**Coconut Sugar:** This sweetener comes from coconut trees and has a yummy caramel taste. It's better for your body because it doesn't make your blood sugar go up as much as regular sugar.

### Smoothie Tip!

You don't need much of these sweeteners—start with a small amount and taste as you go. And remember, fruits like bananas, mangoes, and dates are naturally sweet too!

# THE BEST LIQUIDS FOR YOUR SMOOTHIE CREATIONS

Smoothies need a little liquid to blend everything up to perfection. Here are three great options: water, milk, and juice, with tips on how to prepare them and some awesome lactose-free alternatives for milk.

**Water:** Simple and refreshing, water is a great option when you want to keep things light. You can use regular cold water or step up the flavor with coconut water for a tropical twist. Both keep your smoothie hydrating and clean.

**Tip:**

If you want a smoother texture, use ice-cold water or toss in a couple of ice cubes before blending.

**Milk:** Milk makes your smoothie creamy and rich. But if you're looking for a lactose-free option, here are some delicious alternatives:

- **Almond Milk:** Nutty, light, and dairy-free! Almond milk is a great choice and comes in both sweetened and unsweetened varieties. Be sure to choose the unsweetened kind if you want to keep your smoothie sugar-free.

- **Oat Milk:** This creamy, plant-based milk is made from oats and has a mild flavor that blends well with any smoothie. Plus, it's perfect for anyone with nut allergies!

- **Coconut Milk:** For a rich, tropical twist, coconut milk is your go-to. It adds a slightly sweet and creamy texture—just be sure to use the drinkable coconut milk, not the thick, canned variety!

- **Soy Milk:** Packed with protein, soy milk is another smooth, lactose-free choice. It's a great option if you're looking for something more substantial.

- **Rice Milk:** Light and slightly sweet, rice milk is a gentle option for those with multiple food sensitivities.

**TIP:**

Always shake your plant-based milk before using it to make sure all the goodness is evenly mixed!

**Juice**: it adds sweetness and flavor to your smoothie. But remember, we're all about keeping it natural, so opt for freshly squeezed or cold-pressed juices whenever possible. Here are some popular juice options:

- **Orange Juice:** Bright and zesty, perfect for tropical or fruity smoothies.

- **Apple Juice:** Mild and sweet, a great neutral base for any smoothie.

- **Lime Juice:** Tangy and refreshing, lime juice adds a zippy kick to your smoothie. It's perfect for balancing out the sweeter ingredients, especially in tropical or citrus blends.

**TIP:**

Try to use juice in moderation to avoid adding too much natural sugar. You can even dilute it with water for a lighter option.

# GLUTEN-FREE OPTIONS AND OTHER DIETARY RESTRICTIONS

Most of the liquids mentioned are naturally Gluten-free. However, here's a breakdown:

- **Water & Coconut Water:** Always Gluten-free.

- **Milk:** Traditional cow's milk is Gluten-free, and most plant-based milks are too, but some brands may add thickeners or flavorings that contain gluten

- **Almond Milk, Coconut Milk, Soy Milk, and Rice Milk:** Typically Gluten-free, but as with all products, look for a label that confirms they are certified Gluten-free, just to be safe.

- **Oat Milk:** Not all oat milks are Gluten-free, because oats can sometimes be processed in facilities that handle gluten-containing grains. Always choose oat milk that's labeled Gluten-free.

- **Juice:** Freshly squeezed or 100% pure juices (like orange, apple, or carrot) are naturally Gluten-free. Just avoid any juice mixes with added flavorings or sweeteners that might contain gluten.

## OTHER DIETARY RESTRICTIONS

- **Nut-free Options:** If someone has a nut allergy, avoid almond milk and coconut milk (since coconut can sometimes trigger nut allergies). Great alternatives include oat milk, soy milk, and rice milk.

**Quick reminder:**

check labels!

- **Soy-Free Options:** For anyone avoiding soy, choose options like almond milk, oat milk, coconut milk, or rice milk instead of soy milk.

- **Vegan/Plant-Based:** If you're looking for a completely plant-based option, all of the plant-based milks (almond, oat, coconut, soy, rice milk) are perfect. Juice and water are also vegan-friendly.

**SMOOTHIE TIP!**

Always check for Gluten-free certifications on plant-based milks.

# SMOOTHIE PREP 101

Before you start chopping and slicing, always remember: **ask an adult for help** when using knives or tools! Here are some cool cutting words and prep terms you'll see in our recipes:

## PEEL

This means taking the skin off fruits or veggies. You can peel things like bananas, oranges, or even cucumbers! Use a peeler or your hands, and always get help from an adult for trickier peels.

## SLICE

Slicing means cutting something into flat pieces, like cutting a cucumber into circles or mango into thin strips. Always ask an adult to help hold the knife safely when you slice.

## CHOP

Chopping is cutting things into smaller pieces. You might chop up pineapple chunks or greens like spinach. Remember, chopping can be tricky, so make sure an adult is there to help guide the knife!

## CORE

To core something means taking out the center of fruits like apples or pears, where the seeds are. You can use a tool called an apple corer. Always let an adult do this part.

## HALVE

This just means cutting something in half. You can halve a lemon, peach, or avocado to make it easier to work with. Always let an adult help with the knife for this step.

## SEGMENT

Segmenting is when you cut out the sections of a fruit like an orange or grapefruit, leaving the peel behind. This makes it easy to blend without any tough bits. Let an adult help with segmenting!

## PIT

To pit a fruit means removing the big seed in the middle, like in peaches, cherries, or avocados. Some fruits have tools to make pitting easier, but always ask for help!

## JUICE

Juicing means squeezing the liquid out of fruits like lemons, limes, or oranges. You might use a juicer or just your hands. It's a fun way to get fresh juice, but can get messy, so have an adult show you the best way.

## SMOOTHIE SAFETY TIP:

Remember, knives and graters are sharp! Always ask an adult to help you with any cutting, zesting, or coring in the kitchen. You'll be a pro in no time—with safe hands and tasty smoothies!

# CHAPTER 1

# FRUITYLICIOUS SMOOTHIES

# CHAPTER 1

## FRUITYLICIOUS SMOOTHIES

# FRUITYLICIOUS SMOOTHIES

Fruits are the delightful, colorful gems of the smoothie world, adding natural sweetness and vibrant flavors and colors to every blend. These juicy treasures turn your smoothies into scrumptious delights that are not only tasty but also packed with goodness!

## A Flavor Explosion

Imagine sipping a smoothie bursting with flavors that dance on your tongue! From zesty lemons to sweet mangoes, fruits add a delightful twist that makes every smoothie a tasty adventure. Each sip is like a mini celebration for your taste buds!

## Nutrient-Packed Goodness

Fruits are also loaded with vitamins, minerals, and antioxidants which your body (and your mom and dad) will love. Fruits like bananas and berries provide essential nutrients that help keep your body healthy and strong. So, your smoothie is a yummy treat; plus fuel for your body to power it to thrive!

## Energy to Keep You Going

Fruits are the perfect pick-me-up for any time of day! Unlike sugary snacks that lead to crashes (where you feel lots of energy then feel so tired and yucky), fruits offer a steady supply of energy that keeps you alert and ready for any action that comes your way. Whether you're tackling homework or enjoying playtime, these fruity smoothies give you the boost you need!

# BANANA BLAST!

**Prep Time:** 5-7 minutes
**Yield:** 1 serving

## INGREDIENTS:

- 1 ripe banana
- 1 cup of milk (or dairy-free alternative: almond milk, oat milk, or coconut milk)
- Optional: 1 tbsp of organic honey
- Optional: a handful of ice cubes

## STEPS:

**Prep**: Peel the banana and break it into chunks (you can use your hands!) or grab some frozen banana bites. Measure the milk and get ready to blend.

**Blend**: Add the banana chunks and milk (or milk alternative) to the blender. Secure the lid, and blend on high speed for 25 to 30 seconds until mixed.

**Taste test**: Grab a spoonful of smoothie and taste it. If you want a little more sweetness, you can add your sweetener now. If you'd like your smoothie to be cooler or more refreshing, add a handful of ice cubes before blending again on high speed until smooth and creamy.

**Serve**: Pour into a fun glass, grab a fun straw, and enjoy!

## NUTRITIONAL NOTES!

**Banana Boost**: Packed with potassium to keep your muscles in top shape and fiber to keep your tummy happy.
**Milk Magic**: Milk gives your bones and teeth super strength with its calcium power! And if you go dairy-free, you get a new set of nutrients, like vitamin D and healthy fats, that keep you shining bright and feeling awesome!

Gluten-free

# TROPICAL TWIST: ORANGE & MANGO

**Prep Time:** 5-7 minutes
**Yield:** 1 serving

## INGREDIENTS:

- 1 cup frozen mango chunks (or fresh mangos if you prefer!)
- ½ cup coconut milk
- ½ cup orange juice
- Optional: 1 tbsp of the sweetener of your choice
- Optional: a handful of ice cubes

## STEPS:

**Prep**: If you're using fresh mango instead of frozen, have an adult help you peel it and cut into chunks. Make sure the pieces are small, so they blend easily. Measure the liquids and get blending!

**Blend**: Add the mango chunks, coconut milk, and orange juice into a blender. Secure the lid and blend on high speed for 25 to 30 seconds until mixed.

**Taste test**: Taste a little of your smoothie. If you want more sweetness, add the natural sweetener. You may want to add ice if you used fresh mangos to make it more refreshing. Blend again until smooth and creamy. If it's too thick, add a little more orange juice to thin it out.

**Serve**: Pour into a glass, grab a fun straw, and enjoy!

## NUTRITIONAL NOTES!

**Tropical Vitamin C**: Packed with vitamin C from both mango and orange juice, this smoothie keeps your immune system strong and ready for any adventure!

Gluten-free Dairy-free Nut-free Soy-free Vegan

# BERRYLICIOUS

**Prep Time:** 5-7 minutes
**Yield:** 1 serving

## Ingredients:

- ½ cup strawberries (or frozen strawberries)

- ½ cup blueberries (or frozen blueberries)
- ½ cup of apple juice

## Steps:

**Prep**: If using fresh strawberries, remove the green stems with a knife (make sure to ask an adult for help) or use pre-frozen strawberries. Measure the strawberries and the blueberries. Then, measure the apple juice and get ready to blend.

**Blend**: Add the berries and apple juice into the blender, secure the lid, and blend on high speed for about 25 to 30 seconds.

**Taste test**: Taste your smoothie! If you're using fresh strawberries and you want extra freshness, add a few ice cubes. If the consistency is too thick, add a little more juice and blend until you reach a creamy texture.

**Serve**: Pour the smoothie into a glass and enjoy immediately!

## Nutritional Notes!

**Vitamin Boost**: Berries provide antioxidants, which help protect the body's cells and keep you feeling healthy.

Gluten-free Dairy-free Nut-free Soy-free Vegan

# PEACH PARADISE

**Prep Time:** 5-7 minutes
**Yield:** 1 serving

## INGREDIENTS:

- 1 cup fresh or frozen peach slices
- ½ cup of apple juice
- Optional: a handful of ice cubes

## STEPS:

**Prep**: Measure out 1 cup of frozen peach slices. If you're using fresh peaches, make sure they are peeled, pitted, and sliced beforehand (ask an adult for help with this part). Measure your apple juice and get ready to blend.

**Blend**: Put the peach slices in the blender, add the orange juice for a tangy sweetness. Make sure the blender lid is securely on. Blend for 25 to 30 seconds at high speed.

**Taste test**: Taste your mix. Add ice (if needed) and blend in high speed until smooth and creamy.

**Serve**: Pour into a glass, grab a fun straw, and enjoy!

## NUTRITIONAL NOTES!

**Vitamin C Power-Up**: Peaches and orange juice are packed with vitamin C, giving your immune system a boost and helping keep your skin and body healthy.

Gluten-free Dairy-free Nut-free Soy-free Vegan

# MANGO MELON MAGIC

**Prep Time:** 5–7 minutes
**Yield:** 1 serving

## INGREDIENTS:

- ½ cup mango chunks (frozen mango chunks work too)
- ½ cup cantaloupe chunks (or frozen)
- ½ cup of coconut water
- Optional: a handful of ice cubes

## STEPS:

**Prep**: If you're using fresh mango instead of frozen, have an adult help you peel the mango and cut it into chunks. Cut the cantaloupe too, making sure they are small pieces so they blend easily. Measure your coconut water and get ready to blend!

**Blend**: Combine the chunks in the blender, add coconut water, make sure the lid is securely on, and blend for 25 to 30 seconds until mixed.

**Taste test**: Taste your smoothie, add ice (if you didn't use the frozen chunks), and blend for a few more seconds until smooth and creamy.

**Serve**: Pour into a glass, grab a fun straw, and enjoy the tropical flavor!

## NUTRITIONAL NOTES!

**Vitamin Boost**: Mango and cantaloupe are rich in vitamin A, giving you healthy skin and good vision.

Gluten-free Dairy-free Nut-free Soy-free Vegan

# BANANA BERRY SWIRL

**Prep Time: 5-7 minutes**
**Yield: 1 serving**

## INGREDIENTS:

- ½ banana
- ½ cup frozen raspberries (or fresh ones)
- ½ cup of almond milk (or any milk alternative)
- Optional: 1 tbsp of the sweetener of your choice
- Optional: a handful of ice cubes

## STEPS:

**Prep**: Peel the banana and break it in half or take some frozen banana bites. Measure the raspberries and almond milk and get ready to blend.

**Blend**: Put the banana, raspberries, and milk into the blender. Make sure the lid is on tight to avoid any spills. Blend on high speed for 25 to 30 seconds.

**Taste test**: Check consistency; if you think the smoothie is too thick, add a little extra milk. If you want a little more sweetness, add your organic sweetener. If you didn't use frozen fruit for this one, you can add some ice cubes and blend until smooth.

**Serve**: Pour into a glass, grab a fun straw, and enjoy! You can also add a few extra berries on top to make it pretty.

## NUTRITIONAL NOTES!

**Vitamin Boost**: Bananas provide potassium, which helps keep your muscles and heart healthy while raspberries are packed with antioxidants that protect your body's cells.

Gluten-free Dairy-free Nut-free Soy-free Vegan

# PINEAPPLE POWER PUNCH

**Prep Time:** 5-7 minutes
**Yield:** 1 serving

## INGREDIENTS:

- ½ cup pineapple chunks (frozen works too!)
- ½ cup banana slices
- ½ cup of coconut milk (or any milk alternative)
- Optional: a splash of orange juice
- Optional: a handful of ice cubes

## STEPS:

**Prep**: If you're using fresh fruit, ask an adult for help To cut the pineapple into chunks. Peel the banana and slice it. If you're using frozen fruit, just measure ½ of each, measure the coconut milk and you're ready for the next step!

**Blend**: Add the fruit chunks to the blender; then add the milk. Secure the lid and blend for around 30 seconds on high speed.

**Taste test**: Check the taste and consistency. If you used fresh fruits, you may want to add ice and keep blending until smooth and creamy.

**Serve**: Pour the smoothie into your favorite glass. You can top it with a slice of pineapple or banana if you like, and don't forget to grab a fun straw!

## NUTRITIONAL NOTES!

**Vitamin Boost**: the combination of pineapple and banana provides a boost of vitamin C; it keeps your immune system strong!
**Energy Boost**: banana gives you potassium for energy and muscle health.

Gluten-free Dairy-free Nut-free Soy-free Vegan

# KIWI KRAZE

**Prep Time:** 5-7 minutes
**Yield:** 1 serving

## INGREDIENTS:

- 1 kiwi
- ½ cup strawberries (or frozen strawberries)
- ½ cup of apple juice

## STEPS:

**Prep**: Peel the kiwi and ask for help to chop it into small pieces. If you're using fresh strawberries, cut off the green part and slice them in half. Measure the strawberries and the apple juice and you're ready for the next step.

**Blend**: Add all the ingredients to the blender, secure the lid, and blend on high speed for around 30 seconds.

**Taste test**: Try a bit of your mix, add ice (if needed), and blend until smooth and creamy.

**Serve**: Serve and enjoy your tangy treat!

## NUTRITIONAL NOTES!

**Vitamin C Power**: kiwis and strawberries are packed with vitamin C, giving your immune system a boost to help fight off colds and keep your skin glowing.
**Fiber Frenzy**: kiwi also brings fiber, supporting healthy digestion.

Gluten-free Dairy-free Nut-free Soy-free Vegan

# GRAPEFRUIT BERRY BREEZE

**Prep Time:** 5-7 minutes
**Yield:** 1 serving

## INGREDIENTS:

- ½ grapefruit
- ½ cup frozen raspberries
- ½ cup of water

- Optional: 1 tbsp of the sweetener of your choice
- Optional: a handful of ice cubes

## STEPS:

**Prep**: Peel the grapefruit and separate it into segments. Ask an adult for help because grapefruits can be tricky to peel. Measure your raspberries and water. Get ready to blend!

**Blend**: Add the segments, raspberries, and water into the blender. Secure the lid and blend for about 30 seconds.

**Taste test**: Test a little of your mix, if you feel like it needs to be more refreshing, add a few ice cubes. If you'd like it a little sweeter, add a sweetener. Blend until everything is mixed.

**Serve**: Pour into a glass, grab a cute straw, and enjoy!

## NUTRITIONAL NOTES!

**Vitamin C Power**: Both grapefruit and raspberries are packed with vitamin C, boosting your immune system and keeping your skin healthy.
**Hydration Helper**: The water content in grapefruit helps to keep you hydrated, while raspberries provide antioxidants that help you stay healthy.

Gluten-free Dairy-free Nut-free Soy-free Vegan

# MANGO FUSION

**Prep Time:** 5-7 minutes
**Yield:** 1 serving

## INGREDIENTS:

- ½ cup peach slices (fresh or frozen)
- ½ cup mango chunks (fresh or frozen)
- ½ cup of coconut water

## STEPS:

**Prep**: Measure out frozen peach slices and mango chunks. If you have fresh fruits, ask an adult for help when peeling and cutting. Measure the coconut water and have everything ready to blend.

**Blend**: Add your ingredients to the blender, secure the lid, and blend at high speed for about 25 seconds.

**Taste test**: Check the texture, if it's too thick, add more coconut water. Add ice if you used fresh fruit to ensure extra freshness. Blend for a few more seconds until smooth.

**Serve**: Pour and enjoy the tropical flavors!

## NUTRITIONAL NOTES!

**Tropical Vitamin A & C**: Peaches and mango give you high amounts of vitamins A and C, helping to keep your eyes healthy and boost your immune system.
**Energy Booster**: The natural sugars in these fruits give you a quick and healthy energy boost.

Gluten-free Dairy-free Nut-free Soy-free Vegan

# WATERMELON MINT SWIRL

**Prep Time: 5–7 minutes**
**Yield: 1 serving**

## INGREDIENTS:

- ½ cup watermelon chunks
- ¼ cup fresh mint leaves
- ½ cup of coconut water
- Optional: a handful of ice cubes

## STEPS:

**Prep**: Cut the watermelon into bite-sized chunks (ask an adult for help when using knives). Rinse the mint leaves under cold water. Measure all the ingredients, and get ready to blend.

**Blend**: Add the watermelon, mint, and coconut water to the blender. Make sure the lid is secured and blend at high speed for about 25 seconds.

**Taste test**: Taste your mix, and make sure the mint is mixed throughout. You can add a few ice cubes if you want it extra cold.

**Serve**: Pour into a glass and refresh with this cool, minty treat!

## NUTRITIONAL NOTES!

**Hydration Hero**: Watermelon is made up of over 90% water, helping to keep you hydrated, especially on hot days.
**Minty Freshness**: Mint adds a refreshing flavor and helps you to digest food, making this smoothie both delicious and good for your tummy.

Gluten-free Dairy-free Nut-free Soy-free Vegan

# KIWI PEACH PUNCH

**Prep Time:** 5-7 minutes
**Yield:** 1 serving

## INGREDIENTS:

- 1 kiwi
- ½ cup peach chunks (fresh or frozen)
- ½ cup of orange juice

## STEPS:

**Prep**: Peel and chop the kiwi with an adult's help. If using fresh peaches, slice them into smaller pieces, or measure out frozen peach chunks. Roll an orange on the counter to soften it, then cut it in half and squeeze ½ cup of orange juice.

**Blend**: Add the kiwi, peach slices, and juice into the blender. Mix at high speed for about 25 seconds until mixed.

**Taste test**: Check the consistency, you can add a little more juice if too thick and ice cubes if you want your smoothie extra refreshing. Blend until smooth.

**Serve**: Pour into your favorite glass and enjoy this tangy, fruity punch!

## NUTRITIONAL NOTES!

**Vitamin C Boost**: Kiwi and orange juice are rich in vitamin C, which helps your immune system and gives you glowing skin.
**Peach Power**: Peaches give you vitamin A, which is good for your eyes and overall health.

Gluten-free Dairy-free Nut-free Soy-free Vegan

# TROPICAL TANGO!

**Prep Time:** 5–7 minutes
**Yield:** 1 serving

## INGREDIENTS:

- ½ cup pineapple chunks (fresh or frozen)
- ½ cup mango chunks (fresh or frozen)
- ½ cup of coconut water
- Optional: a handful of ice cubes

## STEPS:

**Prep**: If you're using fresh fruit, peel and chop into chunks. (Remember to ask for help from an adult when using knives.) For a quicker option, you can use frozen fruit. Measure the fruits and the coconut water.

**Blend**: Add the pineapple, mango, and coconut water to the blender. Secure the lid and blend at high speed for 25 to 30 seconds until mixed.

**Taste test**: Check the consistency, and add a little more coconut water if it's too thick. If you used fresh fruits, add some ice cubes for extra refreshment.

**Serve**: Pour into a glass and enjoy immediately for a refreshing tropical treat!

## NUTRITIONAL NOTES!

**Tropical Delight**: Pineapple and mango are packed with vitamins and minerals, while coconut water gives you hydration and electrolytes.
**Vitamin Boost**: This smoothie supports overall health with its high vitamin content and hydrating properties.

Gluten-free Dairy-free Nut-free Soy-free Vegan

# BANANA BONANZA

**Prep Time:** 5-7 minutes
**Yield:** 1 serving

## INGREDIENTS:

- ½ cup blueberries (fresh or frozen)
- 1 banana
- ½ of cup almond milk

- Optional: 1 tbsp of the sweetener of your choice
- Optional: a handful of ice cubes

## STEPS:

**Prep**: Peel and slice the banana in small bits. Remember to ask for help from an adult when using knives. Measure the blueberries and the almond milk. Get ready to blend!

**Blend**: Add the fruit and almond milk to the blender. Secure the lid and blend at high speed for about 25 seconds.

**Taste test**: Check the consistency and add more almond milk if too thick. If you used fresh fruits, add a few ice cubes to cool it. If you need more sweetness, add the sweetener of your choice. Blend until everything is smooth and combined.

**Serve**: Pour into a glass and enjoy immediately for a fruity, delicious treat!

## NUTRITIONAL NOTES!

**Berry Goodness**: Blueberries are rich in antioxidants and vitamins, while bananas give you potassium and natural sweetness!
**Almond Milk Advantage**: Almond milk adds a creamy texture without dairy, perfect for a light, tasty smoothie.

Gluten-free Dairy-free Vegan

# CITRUS BERRY SPLASH

**Prep Time:** 7-15 minutes
**Yield:** 1 serving

## INGREDIENTS:

- 1 orange
- ½ cup strawberries
- ¼ cup blueberries
- ½ cup of coconut water

- Optional: 1 tbsp of the sweetener of your choice
- Optional: a handful of ice cubes

## STEPS:

**Prep**: With an adult's help, peel and segment the orange. Then, take out the green part of the strawberries and cut them in half. Next, measure the ingredients so they're ready for blending.

**Blend**: Add the orange segments, strawberries, blueberries, and coconut water to the blender. Secure the lid and mix!

**Taste test**: Try your mix and add more coconut water if needed. You can add ice and a sweetener if you need, and blend until smooth and creamy.

**Serve**: Pour into a glass and enjoy this refreshing, citrusy berry blend!

## NUTRITIONAL NOTES!

**Citrus Boost**: Oranges are packed with vitamin C, while strawberries and blueberries add antioxidants and flavor.
**Hydration Helper**: Coconut water provides a light, hydrating base for this vibrant smoothie.

Gluten-free Dairy-free Nut-free Soy-free Vegan

# MANGO PINEAPPLE BLITZ

**Prep Time:** 7-15 minutes
**Yield:** 1 serving

## INGREDIENTS:

- ½ cup mango chunks
- ½ cup pineapple chunks
- ½ banana
- ½ cup of almond milk
- Optional: a handful of ice cubes

## STEPS:

**Prep**: Peel and slice the banana. Remember to ask for help from an adult when using knives. If using fresh mango and pineapple, peel and chop into chunks. Next, measure the ingredients so they're ready for blending.

**Blend**: Add the fruit and almond milk to the blender.

**Taste test**: Taste your mix. Adjust by adding more almond milk if needed. Add a few ice cubes for extra coolness.

**Serve**: Pour into a glass and enjoy this tropical, fruity smoothie!

## NUTRITIONAL NOTES!

**Tropical Twist**: Mango and pineapple are full of vitamins and natural sweetness, while banana adds creaminess.
**Almond Milk Advantage**: Almond milk adds a smooth, dairy-free base with a touch of nuttiness.

Gluten-free Dairy-free Vegan

# BERRY MELON MIXER

**Prep Time:** 7-15 minutes
**Yield:** 1 serving

## INGREDIENTS:

- ½ cup watermelon cubes
- ¼ cup blackberries
- ¼ cup strawberries
- ½ cup of lime juice
- Optional: a handful of ice cubes

## STEPS:

**Prep**: With an adult's help, cut the watermelon into cubes and measure out ½ cup. Take out the green part of the strawberries and slice in half. Roll the lime to soften, then cut it in half and squeeze ½ cup of juice. Now, you're ready for blending.

**Blend**: Add the fruit and lime juice to the blender. Make sure the lid is securely on and mix for around 25 to 30 seconds until mixed.

**Taste test**: If the smoothie is too thick, add a little water. Add ice cubes if you want it to be extra cold.

**Serve**: Pour into a glass and enjoy this refreshing, fruity mix!

## NUTRITIONAL NOTES!

**Melon Magic**: Watermelon is hydrating and full of vitamins, while blackberries and strawberries offer antioxidants and flavor.
**Citrus Zing**: Lime juice adds a tangy kick and enhances the natural sweetness of the fruit.

Gluten-free Dairy-free Nut-free Soy-free Vegan

# PEACHY CITRUS SWIRL

**Prep Time: 7-15 minutes**
**Yield: 1 serving**

## INGREDIENTS:

- ½ peach
- ½ orange
- ½ banana

- ½ cup of coconut water
- Optional: a handful of ice cubes

## STEPS:

**Prep**: Peel and slice the peach and banana. Ask for help from an adult when using knives. Peel and segment the orange. Now, measure the coconut water and ingredients so they're ready for blending.

**Blend**: Add the fruit and coconut water to the blender. Secure the lid and mix for 25 to 30 seconds until mixed.

**Taste test**: Try your mix and adjust the consistency by adding more coconut water if needed. You can add ice cubes if you like your smoothies extra cold. Blend until smooth and creamy.

**Serve**: Pour into a glass, add a fun straw, and enjoy this delicious, tropical smoothie!

## NUTRITIONAL NOTES!

**Citrus Peach Perfection**: Peaches and oranges are rich in vitamins A and C, while bananas add creaminess and natural sweetness.
**Potassium Punch**: Bananas are an excellent source of potassium, which is great for your heart and muscle function.
**Hydrating Coconut Water**: Provides a refreshing and hydrating base for this fruity blend.

Gluten-free Dairy-free Nut-free Soy-free Vegan

# RAINBOW FRUIT EXPLOSION!

**Prep Time:** 7-15 minutes
**Yield:** 1 serving

## INGREDIENTS:

- ½ kiwi
- ½ cup mango chunks
- ¼ cup raspberries

- ¼ cup pineapple chunks
- ½ cup of coconut water
- Optional: a handful of ice cubes

## STEPS:

**Prep**: With an adult's help, peel and chop the kiwi, peel the mango, and cut half into little chunks. Cut the pineapple into chunks. Get the coconut water and get ready for blending.

**Blend**: Add the fruit and coconut water to the blender. Secure the lid so there are no spills and mix for 20 to 30 seconds until mixed.

**Taste test**: Adjust the consistency by adding a more coconut water. Add ice if you like, too. Blend until smooth and creamy.

**Serve**: Pour into a fun glass and enjoy this vibrant, fruity smoothie!

## NUTRITIONAL NOTES!

**Fruit Fusion**: Kiwi, mango, raspberries, and pineapple are rich in vitamins and antioxidants, giving you a burst of flavor and nutrition.
**Hydrating Coconut Water**: Adds a refreshing base and helps balance the fruit flavors.

Gluten-free Dairy-free Nut-free Soy-free Vegan

# BERRY CITRUS CRUSH

**Prep Time:** 7–15 minutes
**Yield:** 1 serving

## INGREDIENTS:

- ¼ cup blueberries
- ¼ cup raspberries
- ½ grapefruit
- ¼ cup of orange juice

## STEPS:

**Prep**: With an adult's help, peel and segment half of the grapefruit. Roll the orange to soften it, then cut it in half and squeeze ¼ cup of juice. Measure out the blueberries and raspberries ready for blending.

**Blend**: Add the fruit and orange juice to the blender. Secure the lid and mix for about 25 seconds until combined.

**Taste test**: Try your mix, check the consistency, add a little water if needed. If you want some extra coldness, add ice cubes and keep blending!

**Serve**: Pour into a glass and enjoy this tangy, fruity smoothie!

## NUTRITIONAL NOTES!

**Berry Power**: Blueberries and raspberries are packed with antioxidants and vitamins.
**Citrus Boost**: Grapefruit and orange juice provide a vitamin C kick and a burst of refreshing flavor.

Gluten-free Dairy-free Nut-free Soy-free Vegan

# BONUS:
# LET'S ADD YOGURT!

# CREAMY BERRY DELIGHT

**Prep Time:** 5 minutes
**Yield:** 1 serving

## INGREDIENTS:

- 1/2 cup mixed berries (strawberries, blueberries, raspberries)
- 1/2 ripe banana
- 1/2 cup yogurt (plain or vanilla)
- 1/2 cup of apple juice
- Optional: a handful of ice cubes

## STEPS:

**Prep**: Wash the berries thoroughly. If using a knife to slice the banana, ask for help from an adult. For the best flavor, use organic fresh fruit when possible, but frozen fruit is also fine.

**Blend**: In a blender, combine the fruit, yogurt, and apple juice. Mix at a high speed for around 25 seconds.

**Taste test**: Taste your mix, if the smoothie is too thick, add a more apple juice. Add ice if you want extra refreshment!

**Serve**: Pour the smoothie into a glass and enjoy immediately.

## NUTRITIONAL NOTES!

**Protein Power-Up**: Yogurt offers protein and probiotics that are excellent for muscle growth and gut health.
**Antioxidant Heroes**: Berries are packed with antioxidants, vitamins C and K, helping to boost immunity and promote healthy skin.
**Banana Boost**: Bananas provide potassium for heart health and natural sweetness to keep your smoothie delicious.
**Juicy Goodness**: Apple juice adds a touch of sweetness and provides additional vitamins to keep you energized.

Gluten-free Nut-free Soy-Free
*Use a plant-based yogurt alternative for a dairy-free version

# KIWI BANANA CREAM

**Prep Time:** 5 minutes
**Yield:** 1 serving

## INGREDIENTS:

- 1 ripe kiwi
- 1/2 ripe banana
- 1/2 cup yogurt (vanilla or plain)
- 1/2 cup of almond milk
- Optional: 1 tbsp of organic honey
- Optional: a handful of ice cubes

## STEPS:

**Prep**: Ask for an adult's help to peel and chop the kiwis and slice the banana. Use organic fresh fruit when possible, but frozen fruit is also good!

**Blend**: In a blender, combine the kiwis, banana, yogurt, and almond milk. Mix for 20 to 25 seconds at high speed, and remember: always make sure the lid is securely on to avoid spills.

**Taste test**: Try your mix, if you prefer a thinner consistency, add more milk. You can also add ice to cool it down. Add a tablespoon of organic honey for more sweetness.

**Serve**: Pour the smoothie into a glass, grab a fun straw, and enjoy!

## NUTRITIONAL NOTES!

**Kiwi Kick**: Kiwis are rich in vitamin C, vitamin K, and dietary fiber, supporting immune health and digestion.
**Banana Boost**: Bananas provide potassium and natural sweetness, enhancing the flavor and provide lots of nutrition.
**Yogurt Yum**: Yogurt adds a creamy texture and beneficial probiotics for a healthy gut!
**Almond Milk Magic**: Almond milk is a low-calorie alternative to dairy, giving a nutty flavor and vitamin E.

Gluten-free
*If you're looking for vegan options, try using a plant-based yogurt

# BERRY CITRUS YOGURT SHAKE

**Prep Time:** 5 minutes
**Yield:** 1 serving

## INGREDIENTS:

- 1/2 cup strawberries
- 1/2 cup blueberries
- 1/2 cup yogurt (plain or vanilla)
- 1/2 cup of grapefruit juice
- Optional: a handful of ice cubes

## STEPS:

**Prep**: With an adult's help, cut off the green part of the strawberries and slice in half. Roll a grapefruit to soften it, then squeeze ½ cup of juice. Measure out the berries, the yogurt and have them ready to blend.

**Blend**: In a blender, combine the fruit, yogurt, and juice. Secure the lid and mix for around 25 to 30 seconds until smooth.

**Taste test**: Try your mix, if the smoothie is too thick, you can add juice. Add ice if to make it refreshing, and blend for a few seconds until everything is perfectly mixed.

**Serve**: Pour the smoothie into a pretty glass and enjoy!

## NUTRITIONAL NOTES!

**Berry Boost**: Strawberries and blueberries are packed with antioxidants, vitamins C and K, supporting both immune and skin health.
**Yogurt Yum**: Yogurt adds a creamy texture and beneficial probiotics for gut health.
**Citrus Zing**: Grapefruit juice provides a refreshing flavor and is rich in vitamin C, helping to boost your immune system.

Gluten-free Nut-free
*If you're looking for vegan options, try using a plant-based yogurt

# APPLE PEAR YOGURT SMOOTHIE

**Prep Time:** 5 minutes
**Yield:** 1 serving

## INGREDIENTS:

- 1/2 apple
- 1/2 pear
- 1/2 cup yogurt (plain or vanilla)
- 1/4 teaspoon cinnamon
- 1/4 cup of water or apple juice
- Optional: a handful of ice cubes

## STEPS:

**Prep**: With an adult's help, peel and chop the fruit by cutting them into small pieces so they're easy to blend. Measure out the yogurt and juice or water and get ready to blend!

**Blend**: Add the chopped fruit, yogurt, cinnamon, and water (or apple juice) into a blender. Secure the lid. Mix for around 20 seconds at high speed.

**Taste test**: taste and adjust by adding more water or juice if needed. You can add ice too. Blend until smooth and creamy.

**Serve**: Pour into your favorite glass, grab a straw, and enjoy!

## NUTRITIONAL NOTES!

**Fiber Power**: This smoothie is loaded with fiber from the apple and pear, supporting healthy digestion.
**Probiotic Punch**: Yogurt provides probiotics that help keep your gut happy and healthy.
**Antioxidant Boost**: Cinnamon adds antioxidants and a touch of natural sweetness, making it a perfect addition.

Nut-free Soy-free
*Try using a plant-based yogurt for a vegan option

# RASPBERRY LIME YOGURT SMOOTHIE

**Yield:** 1 serving
**Prep Time:** 5 minutes

## INGREDIENTS:

- 1/2 cup raspberries (fresh or frozen)
- 1/2 cup yogurt (plain or vanilla)
- 1/4 cup lime juice
- 1/4 cup of coconut water (or regular water)
- Optional: 1 tbsp of the sweetener of your choice
- Optional: a handful of ice cubes

## STEPS:

**Prep**: With an adult's help, cut a lime in half and squeeze ¼ cup of its juice. Measure out the raspberries, yogurt, and coconut water ready to blend.

**Blend**: Add the raspberries and liquids to the blender, making sure the lid is securely on. Blend on high speed until smooth and creamy.

**Taste test**: Try your mix. Adjust sweetness by adding your sweetener of choice (always go for an organic option!) and add some ice if you need. Blend for a few seconds and ta-da!

**Serve**: Pour the marvelous mix into a glass and drink it fresh.

## NUTRITIONAL NOTES!

**Berry Boost**: Raspberries are high in fiber and antioxidants, helping with digestive health and immunity.
**Creamy Delight**: Yogurt adds a creamy texture and lots of probiotics for gut health.

Nut-free Soy-free
*Try using a plant-based yogurt for a vegan option

# CHAPTER 2

# VEGGIE SMOOTHIES

# VEGGIE SMOOTHIES

I know what you're thinking—"Veggies in my smoothie? No way!" But hang tight, I'm going to show you that veggies aren't just for boring dinners—they're the secret ingredients to becoming a healthy smoothie-making master!

## GET NUTRITIOUS HIDDEN POWERS

Veggies are packed with vitamins and minerals that help you grow tall, keep your bones strong, and your mind super sharp! Leafy greens like spinach and kale are full of iron and calcium, while bright-colored veggies like carrots and beets are loaded with vitamins that help you see better, feel better, and even fight off those pesky germs. Adding veggies is an easy way to get all these benefits without even realizing it!

## KEEP YOUR TUMMY HEALTHY AND HAPPY

They are full of fiber, which works like a broom inside your body, sweeping away anything that shouldn't be there. When you have enough fiber, you feel good, your tummy doesn't feel stuck or too full, and you're ready for more fun and play! Adding vegetables like carrots, zucchini, or spinach to your smoothies is a tasty way to make sure you're getting enough fiber without even thinking about it.

## BOOST YOUR ENERGY

Veggies give you the kind of energy that lasts! Unlike candies that give you a quick burst of energy and then leave you feeling sleepy or grumpy, veggies help keep your energy going strong all day. They help you stay focused in school, power through your homework and still have energy left for fun with friends. With yummy smoothie blends, you get the best of both worlds—delicious flavors and long-lasting veggie power!

# SWEET SPINACH SURPRISE

**Prep Time:** 5-7 minutes
**Yield:** 1 serving

## INGREDIENTS:

- 1 cup fresh spinach (or ½ cup of frozen spinach)
- 1 ripe banana
- ½ cup pineapple chunks (fresh or frozen)

- 1 cup of coconut water
- Optional: 1 tbsp of the sweetener of your choice
- Optional: a handful of ice cubes

## STEPS:

**Prep**: If you're using fresh spinach, make sure it's washed and dried. Peel the banana and cut it into chunks. Remember to ask for help from an adult when using knives. If you're using frozen spinach, you can skip the washing. Measure the pineapple chunks and coconut water.

**Blend**: Add the spinach, banana, and pineapple into the blender. Pour in the coconut water. Secure the lid and blend for 25 to 30 seconds until mixed

**Taste test**: Try the mix, if it's too thick, add a little more coconut water. Add a sweetener of your choice, making sure to use natural options. You can also add ice to cool it.

**Serve**: Pour the smoothie into a glass or a fun cup. You can use colorful straws to make it extra colorful and fun to drink!

## NUTRITIONAL NOTES!

**Iron Power**: Spinach helps you stay strong and energetic!
**Vitamin C Boost**: Pineapple gives your immune system a superhero upgrade!
**Fiber Fun**: Bananas and spinach keep your tummy happy and healthy.

Gluten-free Dairy-free Nut-free Soy-free

# AVOCADO GREEN SMOOTHIE

**Prep Time:** 5-7 minutes
**Yield:** 1 serving

## INGREDIENTS:

- ½ avocado
- 1 cup fresh kale
- 1 small green apple
- 1 tablespoon of lime juice

- 1 cup of coconut milk
- Optional: 1 tbsp of the sweetener of your choice
- Optional: a handful of ice cubes

## STEPS:

**Prep**: With an adult's help, cut the avocado in half and scoop out the flesh of one half. Core and slice the apple. Roll the lime to soften it, then cut it in half and squeeze 1 tablespoon of juice. Measure out the kale and coconut milk.

**Blend**: Add the avocado, kale, apple, and juice to the blender. Pour in the coconut milk. Secure the lid and blend for 25 to 30 seconds.

**Taste test**: Check if the smoothie is too thick, and add a little coconut milk. Add the natural sweetener, a few ice cubes, and blend until smooth.

**Serve**: Pour into a glass and enjoy this creamy, healthy, green smoothie!

## NUTRITIONAL NOTES!

**Healthy Fats**: Avocado provides creamy texture and healthy fats to keep you full and satisfied and less likely to want to snack.
**Fiber Boost**: Spinach and apple add fiber to help with digestion.
**Vitamin C Kick**: Lime juice adds a zesty flavor and vitamin C to help out your immune system.

Gluten-free Dairy-free Nut-free Soy-free.

# CARROT MANGO SPLASH

**Prep Time:** 7-10 minutes
**Yield:** 1 serving

## Ingredients:

- ½ cup of orange juice (or water)
- ½ medium carrot
- ½ ripe mango
- ¼ banana
- Optional: 1 teaspoon of organic honey or maple syrup
- Optional: a handful of ice cubes

## Steps:

**Prep**: With the help of an adult, peel and chop the carrot and mango. Peel the banana and grab ¼ for this smoothie. Measure ½ cup of orange juice.

**Blend**: Blend the juice and carrot until smooth. Add the mango, banana, and organic honey/maple syrup.

**Taste test**: Try your mix and adjust sweetness by adding more sweetener and thickness by adding ice. Keep blending until smooth.

**Serve**: Pour the smoothie into your favorite cup, grab a straw, and enjoy this healthy drink!

## Nutritional Notes!

**Vitamin Power-Up**: Carrots and orange juice are loaded with vitamin A and vitamin C, helping boost your immune system and keep your eyes sharp!
**Tropical Twist**: Mango brings a sweet tropical flavor and adds fiber to keep you feeling full and happy.
**Energy Boost**: That small bit of banana gives you a quick energy boost with natural sugars, making this smoothie a perfect power-up!

Gluten-free Dairy-free Nut-free Vegan

# BERRY BEET BOOST

**Prep Time:** 5-7 minutes
**Yield:** 1 serving

## INGREDIENTS:

- ¼ small cooked beetroot
- ½ cup mixed berries (strawberries, blueberries, or raspberries)
- ¼ cup yogurt (Greek or dairy-free)
- ¼ cup of almond milk (or milk of choice)
- Optional: ½ tablespoon chia seeds
- Optional: ½ tablespoon honey
- Optional: a handful of ice cubes

## STEPS:

**Prep**: With the help of an adult, chop the cooked beetroot. Measure out the berries, yogurt, and almond milk. If you're using chia seeds or honey, have those ready, too!

**Blend**: Start by blending the beetroot, milk, and yogurt until smooth. Add the berries, chia seeds, and honey. Keep blending until smooth.

**Taste test**: Try your mix and adjust sweetness by adding more honey and coolness by adding ice. Keep blending until everything is smooth.

**Serve**: Pour into your favorite cup, pop in a straw, and enjoy your veggie creation!

## NUTRITIONAL NOTES!

**Fiber Boost**: Beetroot and berries pack this smoothie with fiber to keep your tummy happy.
**Antioxidant Blast**: Mixed berries are full of antioxidants to help keep you strong and healthy.
**Protein Power**: The yogurt adds extra protein for energy and muscle strength.

Gluten-free

# GREEN POWER PUNCH

**Prep Time:** 5–7 minutes
**Yield:** 1 serving

## INGREDIENTS:

- ½ cup of coconut water (or water)
- ½ cup chopped cucumber
- ½ small zucchini, chopped
- ¼ ripe banana

- 1 tablespoon peanut butter (or nut/seed butter of choice)
- Optional: ½ tablespoon honey
- Optional: a handful of ice cubes

## STEPS:

**Prep**: With the help of an adult, chop the cucumber and zucchini. Peel and measure ¼ ripe banana. Have your peanut butter and honey ready. Measure your coconut water too.

**Blend**: Blend the coconut water, cucumber, and zucchini until smooth. Add the banana, peanut butter, and honey and blend until the smoothie is creamy and well-mixed. Always make sure the lid of the blender is securely on!

**Taste test**: If it's too thick, add more coconut water. Add ice for extra coolness. Blend and get ready to serve.

**Serve**: Pour into a glass, grab your straw, and power up with your green punch!

## NUTRITIONAL NOTES!

**Hydration Boost**: Coconut water and cucumber are super hydrating, helping you stay refreshed all day long.
**Veggie Power**: Zucchini and cucumber add fiber and vitamins without overpowering the flavor.
**Healthy Fats**: Peanut butter provides a dose of healthy fats and protein for energy and brain power!

Gluten-free Dairy-free

# PUMPKIN SPICE SMOOTHIE

**Prep Time:** 5-7 minutes
**Yield:** 1 serving

## INGREDIENTS:

- ½ cup pumpkin puree (canned or fresh)
- 1 ripe banana
- 1 cup of unsweetened almond milk
- ½ teaspoon cinnamon
- Optional: 1 teaspoon pure maple syrup
- Optional: a handful of ice cubes

## STEPS:

**Prep**: With the help of an adult, measure ½ cup of pumpkin puree, then peel and slice the banana. Have your almond milk, cinnamon, and maple syrup ready.

**Blend**: In a blender, combine the pumpkin puree, banana, almond milk, and cinnamon. If you like it sweet, add the maple syrup. Blend until smooth and creamy. Always make sure the lid of the blender is securely on!

**Taste test**: Check the consistency. If too thick, add more almond milk. Add ice for extra chill. Blend for a few more seconds and get ready to serve.

**Serve**: Pour into a glass, grab your straw, and enjoy your pumpkin spice goodness!

## NUTRITIONAL NOTES!

**Vitamin Boost**: Pumpkin is rich in vitamins A and C, providing antioxidants to support your health.
**Creamy Delight**: The banana adds natural sweetness and creaminess without the need for additional sugar.
**Hydrating & Nourishing**: Almond milk is a low-calorie, dairy-free alternative, making this smoothie both hydrating and nutritious!

Gluten-free Dairy-free

# CUCUMBER MELON COOLER

Prep Time: 5-7 minutes
Yield: 1 serving

- 1 small cucumber
- 1 cup honeydew melon
- 1 tablespoon fresh mint leaves
- 1 tablespoon of lime juice

- Optional: 1-2 teaspoons of organic honey
- Optional: a handful of ice cubes

**prep**  Wash the cucumber, peel the cucumber and melon. Measure out the lime juice and honey. Pick your mint leaves and set aside.

**blend**  In a blender, combine the cucumber, honeydew melon, mint leaves, lime juice, and honey (if desired) for a relish. If using ice, add the ice cubes. Blend until smooth and frothy. Always make sure the lid of the blender is securely on!

**taste test**  Check the flavor. If you want it sweeter, add a bit more honey and blend again. If you would prefer it more tart...

**serve**  Pour into glasses, top with mint sprigs, and enjoy your cool and refreshing drink!

# CUCUMBER MELON COOLER

**Prep Time:** 5-7 minutes
**Yield:** 1 serving

## INGREDIENTS:

- ½ small cucumber
- 1 cup honeydew melon
- 1 tablespoon fresh mint leaves
- 1 tablespoon of lime juice
- Optional: 1-2 teaspoons of organic honey
- Optional: a handful of ice cubes

## STEPS:

**Prep**: With the help of an adult, chop the cucumber and melon. Measure out the lime juice and have your mint leaves and honey ready.

**Blend**: In a blender, combine the cucumber, honeydew melon, mint leaves, lime juice, and honey (if desired). For a refreshing cooler, add a handful of ice cubes. Blend until smooth and frothy. Always make sure the lid of the blender is securely on!

**Taste test**: Check the flavor. If it needs more sweetness, add more honey and blend again. If you want it colder, add more ice.

**Serve**: Pour into glasses, top with a sprig of mint, and enjoy your cool and refreshing drink!

## NUTRITIONAL NOTES!

**Hydration Hero**: Cucumber and honeydew melon are both hydrating, making this smoothie perfect for warm days.
**Minty Freshness**: The mint adds a refreshing twist that enhances the flavors and helps with digestion.
**Vitamin C Boost**: Honeydew melon is rich in vitamin C, supporting your immune system and skin health

Gluten-free Dairy-Free

# CARROT CAKE SMOOTHIE

**Prep Time: 5 – 7 minutes**
**Yield: 1 cup**

## INGREDIENTS:

- 1 cup of carrot juice
- 1 ripe banana
- ¼ cup rolled oats
- ½ teaspoon cinnamon

- ½ cup Greek yogurt (or dairy-free yogurt)
- Optional: 1 teaspoon of pure maple syrup
- Optional: a handful of ice cubes

## STEPS:

**Prep**: With the help of an adult, measure out 1 cup of carrot juice, peel and slice the banana, and measure ¼ cup of rolled oats. Have your yogurt, cinnamon, and maple syrup ready.

**Blend**: In a blender, combine carrot juice, banana, rolled oats, cinnamon, and yogurt. If you like it a bit sweeter, add maple syrup. Blend until smooth and creamy, ensuring the lid of the blender is securely on!

**Taste test**: Check the consistency; if it's too thick, add more carrot juice. For a colder smoothie, add ice and blend a little more.

**Serve**: Pour into a glass, grab your straw, and be surprised with the delicious flavors of carrot cake!

## NUTRITIONAL NOTES!

**Fiber Power**: Rolled oats and bananas provide lots of dietary fiber for healthy digestion.
**Vitamin A Boost**: Carrot juice is rich in vitamin A, which supports eye health and boosts the immune system.
**Protein Punch**: Greek yogurt adds protein, making this smoothie a satisfying snack or breakfast option.

Soy-Free Dairy-free: Substitute Greek yogurt with a plant-based yogurt for a dairy-free option
Gluten-free: Ensure to use gluten-free oats for those avoiding gluten

# CHAPTER 3

# SUPER SMOOTHIE BOWLS!

# SUPER SMOOTHIE BOWLS!

Welcome to the chapter of **smoothie bowls**—a magical place where smoothies are so thick and tasty, you eat them with a spoon! Smoothie bowls are perfect for breakfast, a snack, or any time you want a yummy treat that's both healthy and fun to make.

Here's what makes smoothie bowls so special:

**Thick & Creamy:** Smoothie bowls are like a super thick smoothie! The trick? Use less liquid and more frozen fruit or veggies to get that perfect spoon-worthy texture.

**Topping Time!** This is where the fun really begins! Load up your smoothie bowl with all kinds of toppings like crunchy granola, fresh fruit, nuts, seeds, or even a swirl of peanut butter. The best part? You get to mix and match!

**Balanced & Yummy:** Not only are smoothie bowls fun, but they're also packed with goodies to keep you feeling full and strong. Add ingredients that give you a mix of protein (like yogurt or peanut butter), fiber (like fruit and oats), and healthy fats (like avocado or chia seeds)!

**Get Creative!** Making a smoothie bowl is like being an artist—create your own edible masterpiece with bright, colorful toppings. Try to arrange them in fun patterns, like smiley faces or rainbows.

**Mix It Up:** Don't be afraid to experiment. You can use any fruits, veggies, or toppings you love! Want a tropical bowl? Go for pineapple and coconut. Feeling like a chocolatey treat? Add some cacao nibs and bananas!

Are you ready to grab your spoon and dive into a delicious, colorful, and super fun smoothie bowl? Let's get started!

# FUN TOPPINGS AND SUPER NUTRITIONAL BOOSTS

Smoothie bowls are a fun way to explore new flavors and textures. Adding toppings not only makes them more exciting but also boosts their nutrition. Here are some tasty and fun options:

## 1. Fresh Fruit

Fresh fruit like berries, banana slices, and kiwi add sweetness and color to smoothie bowls. They're full of vitamins and fiber, making them a healthy and delicious choice.

**Nutritional boost:** Vitamins C and A, fiber, antioxidants

## 2. Nuts and Seeds

Almonds, chia seeds, and sunflower seeds give a great crunch and provide healthy fats and protein. For younger kids, use finely chopped nuts or ground seeds.

**Nutritional boost:** Omega-3s, healthy fats, protein, fiber

## 3. Granola

A sprinkle of granola adds a delicious punch. Try whole-grain, low-sugar granola for a more nutritious option.

**Nutritional boost:** Whole grains, fiber, iron

## 4. Nut Butters

Almond or peanut butter provides a creamy richness and is a great source of healthy fats and plant-based protein. Choose unsweetened varieties for added health benefits.

**Nutritional boost:** Protein, healthy fats, vitamin E

## 5. Coconut Flakes

Shredded coconut or coconut chips give a tropical touch while adding essential nutrients like iron and fiber.

**Nutritional boost:** Healthy fats, fiber, iron

## 6. Dark Chocolate Chips

A sprinkle of dark chocolate chips adds a sweet treat while adding healthy antioxidants. Make sure you don't add too much!

**Nutritional boost:** Antioxidants, magnesium

## 7. Cinnamon or Spices

A dash of cinnamon or nutmeg can add to the flavor of your smoothie bowl and offer health benefits. Cinnamon, for example, can help with blood sugar regulation.

**Nutritional boost:** Antioxidants, anti-inflammatory properties

**NOTE:**

Always be mindful of allergies when adding nuts, seeds, or any other toppings. Be sure to check for any known sensitivities and change it for safety..

# BERRY BANANA BURST BOWL

**Prep Time: 5 – 7 minutes**
**Yield: 1 bowl**

## INGREDIENTS:

- 1 frozen banana
- ½ cup mixed berries (frozen or fresh strawberries, blueberries, or raspberries)
- ¼ cup almond milk
- ¼ cup yogurt (dairy or dairy-free)
- Optional: one teaspoon of organic honey or pure maple syrup
- Toppings: sliced bananas, chia seeds, fresh blueberries, raspberries

## STEPS:

**Prep & Blend**: If your banana isn't frozen yet, peel it and slice it before freezing. Make sure your mixed berries are washed and ready to go! If using frozen berries, even better! In a blender, add the frozen banana, mixed berries, almond milk, and yogurt. Blend until smooth and creamy. If it's too thick, add a little more almond milk until it's just right.

**Taste & Serve**: Give it a quick taste! If you want it sweeter, add a drizzle of organic honey or maple syrup. Pour the smoothie mixture into your favorite bowl. Get creative with how you present it!

## TOPPING TIME!

- Sliced bananas: for extra sweetness and a yummy look.
- Chia seeds: sprinkle them on for a nutritious boost and a nice crunch.
- Fresh blueberries and raspberries: add these for a pop of color and more berry goodness!

## NUTRITIONAL NOTES!

**Nutrient Boost**: Mixed berries provide antioxidants for immunity, frozen banana adds sweetness, creaminess, and potassium for muscles, and yogurt offers probiotics for digestion.

Gluten-free

# TROPICAL SUNSHINE BOWL

**Prep Time: 5 – 7 minutes**
**Yield: 1 bowl**

## INGREDIENTS:

- ½ cup frozen mango
- ¼ cup pineapple chunks
- ¼ cup of coconut water
- ¼ cup yogurt (dairy or dairy-free)
- Optional: one teaspoon of organic honey or pure maple syrup
- Toppings: coconut flakes, kiwi slices and mango bites, granola

## STEPS:

**Prep & Blend**: If you don't have frozen mango, peel and chop a ripe mango before freezing. Make sure your pineapple is ready to go, fresh or canned (drained). Measure out the coconut water and the yogurt. In a blender, mix the mango, pineapple, coconut water, and yogurt. Blend until smooth and creamy. If you prefer it thinner, add a little more coconut water.

**Taste & Serve**: If you want it sweeter, add a touch of honey or maple syrup, but the natural sweetness from the mango and pineapple is usually enough! Pour the smoothie mixture into your favorite bowl. Make it look extra special with your toppings.

## TOPPING TIME!

- Coconut flakes: sprinkle them on for a tropical touch and added texture.
- Kiwi slices and mango bites: arrange these for a burst of color and flavor.
- Granola: add a handful for crunch and extra nutrients!

## NUTRITIONAL NOTES!

**Tropical Boost**: Mango and pineapple are rich in vitamins A and C for immune support and glowing skin. Coconut water hydrates and provides electrolytes for energy. Yogurt adds gut-friendly probiotics for digestion, while granola offers fiber and healthy fats for lasting energy—just watch out for added sugars in store-bought options.

Gluten-free

# GREEN MONSTER BOWL

**Prep Time:** 5 – 7 minutes
**Yield:** 1 bowl

## INGREDIENTS:

- ½ ripe avocado
- ½ cup spinach leaves
- ½ ripe banana
- ¼ cup of almond milk
- ¼ cup yogurt (dairy or dairy-free)

- Optional: one teaspoon of organic honey or pure maple syrup
- Optional: a handful of ice cubes
- Toppings: banana slices, chia seeds, pumpkin seeds

## STEPS:

**Prep & Blend**: Make sure your avocado is ripe, and your spinach is fresh and washed. Peel the banana and get it ready for blending. In a blender, add the avocado, spinach, banana, almond milk, and yogurt. Blend until smooth and creamy. If too thick, add a bit more almond milk.

**Taste & Serve**: If you want it sweeter, add a drizzle of organic honey or maple syrup, but the banana usually does a great job! For a thicker texture, add a handful of ice cubes and blend to perfection. Pour your smoothie mixture into your favorite bowl, making it look extra appealing with a nice presentation!

## TOPPING TIME!

- Banana: add slices of banana for a burst of color and sweetness.
- Chia seeds: for extra nutrition and crunch.
- Pumpkin seeds: for a nutty flavor and added texture.

## NUTRITIONAL NOTES!

**Nutrient Boost**: Avocado offers healthy fats for heart health and glowing skin, spinach provides vitamins and minerals, including iron for energy, banana adds natural sweetness and potassium for muscle health, and chia and pumpkin seeds contribute fiber, protein, and healthy fats for an extra nutritious bowl!

Gluten-free

# CHOCOLATE DELIGHT BOWL

**Prep Time:** 5 – 7 minutes
**Yield:** 1 bowl

## INGREDIENTS:

- ½ cup frozen banana
- 1 tablespoon unsweetened cocoa powder
- ¼ cup of almond milk
- ¼ cup yogurt (dairy or dairy-free)

- Optional: one teaspoon of organic honey or pure maple syrup
- Toppings: strawberries and sliced bananas, shredded coconut, dark chocolate chips

## STEPS:

**Prep & Blend**: If your banana isn't frozen, peel and slice before freezing. Make sure to have your cocoa powder and almond milk ready for blending. In a blender, combine the banana, cocoa powder, almond milk, and yogurt. Blend until smooth and creamy. If you want it thinner, just add more almond milk.

**Taste & Serve**: If you want it sweeter, add some honey or maple syrup, but the banana is usually enough! Pour the delicious chocolate mixture into your favorite bowl, making it look irresistible!

## TOPPING TIME!

- Sliced strawberries and bananas: for a fruity contrast and extra sweetness.
- Shredded coconut: for a tropical twist.
- Dark chocolate chips: a sprinkle of mini dark chocolate chips for that extra chocolatey goodness.

## NUTRITIONAL NOTES!

**Choco Power**: Cocoa powder is rich in antioxidants to boost your mood. Banana adds natural sweetness and potassium for energy, while yogurt provides probiotics for gut health and creaminess. Mini dark chocolate chips satisfy your sweet tooth with heart-healthy benefits.

Gluten-free

# PEACHY GREEN BOWL

**Prep Time:** 5 – 7 minutes
**Yield:** 1 bowl

## INGREDIENTS:

- ½ ripe peach (fresh or frozen)
- ½ ripe banana
- ½ cup spinach leaves
- ¼ cup of almond milk
- ¼ cup yogurt (dairy or dairy-free)
- Optional: one teaspoon of organic honey or pure maple syrup
- Toppings: strawberries and sliced bananas, shredded coconut, dark chocolate chips

## STEPS:

**Prep & Blend**: If using fresh peaches, ask an adult for help when washing and slicing it. If it's frozen, it's ready to go! Peel the banana, grab half, and break it into smaller chunks. Measure out the spinach, yogurt, almond milk and everything should be ready! In a blender, add the peaches, banana, spinach, almond milk, and yogurt. Blend until smooth and creamy. If the mixture is too thick, add more milk.

**Taste & Serve**: If you like it sweeter, add a little honey or maple syrup, but the banana and peach usually do a great job of sweetening the bowl! Pour the fruity green mixture into your favorite bowl, and enjoy!

## TOPPING TIME!

- Sliced almonds: for a crunchy texture.
- Fresh peach slices for added sweetness and color.
- Organic Honey: add a drizzle of honey or maple syrup for an extra touch of sweetness..

## NUTRITIONAL NOTES!

**Peachy Power**: Peaches provide vitamins A and C for healthy skin and immunity. Spinach adds iron and nutrients for energy, banana offers natural sweetness and potassium for muscle health, and almonds deliver healthy fats and protein for a satisfying crunch.

Gluten-free

# APPLE CINNAMON DELIGHT BOWL

**Prep Time:** 7-10 minutes
**Yield:** 1 bowl

## INGREDIENTS:

- ½ small apple
- ½ ripe banana
- ¼ cup Greek yogurt or dairy-free yogurt
- ¼ cup of almond milk (or milk of choice)
- ½ teaspoon ground cinnamon

- Optional: one teaspoon of organic honey or pure maple syrup
- Optional: a handful of ice cubes
- Toppings: apple slices, granola, cinnamon

## STEPS:

**Prep & Blend**: With an adult's help, peel and chop the apple. Peel the banana and break it into halves. Measure out the rest of the ingredients. In a blender, add the apple, banana, yogurt, almond milk, and cinnamon. Blend it up! If you like it a little, just add more milk. For a thicker and fresh consistency, add ice cubes. Blend until everything is smooth and combined.

**Taste & Serve**: Taste your blend! If you want it sweeter, add organic honey or maple syrup. Pour the apple-cinnamon mixture into your favorite bowl and get ready to top it off!

## TOPPING TIME!

- Thin apple slices: for a fresh crunch.
- Granola: a sprinkle for extra texture a sprinkle of granola.
- Cinnamon: a dash of cinnamon to make the flavors pop!

## NUTRITIONAL NOTES!

**Nutritional Boost**: Apples are high in fiber and vitamin C for immunity and digestion. Cinnamon regulates blood sugar and is rich in antioxidants. Banana adds natural sweetness and potassium for muscle and energy support, while granola provides fiber and healthy fats for a filling bowl.

Gluten-free (if using gluten-free granola)
Dairy-free(if using dairy-free yogurt)
Vegan (if using plant-based yogurt and skipping honey)

# STRAWBERRY COCONUT DREAM BOWL

**Prep Time:** 7-10 minutes
**Yield:** 1 bowl

## INGREDIENTS:

- ½ cup strawberries (fresh or frozen)
- ¼ cup of coconut milk
- ¼ cup Greek yogurt or dairy-free yogurt
- 1 teaspoon maple syrup (optional)

- Optional: one teaspoon of organic honey or pure maple syrup
- Optional: a handful of ice cubes
- Toppings: strawberries, coconut flakes, chia seeds

## STEPS:

**Prep & Blend**: If using fresh strawberries, take out the green part and slice in half. Remember to ask an adult for help when using knives. If they're frozen, they're ready to go! In a blender, add the strawberries, coconut milk, yogurt, and maple syrup. Blend until smooth and creamy. If you want it thinner, add more coconut milk. For a thicker consistency, add ice.

**Taste & Serve**: If you want it sweeter, add maple syrup. Pour the strawberry-coconut mixture into your favorite bowl and get ready to top it off!

## TOPPING TIME!

- Fresh strawberry slices: for a juicy pop.
- Coconut flakes: for a tropical crunch.
- Chia seeds: for added nutrition.

## NUTRITIONAL NOTES!

**Berry Bliss**: Strawberries are high in vitamin C and antioxidants for immune support. Coconut milk adds creaminess and healthy fats for satisfaction, while chia seeds provide fiber, omega-3s, and protein for an energy boost!

Gluten-free
Dairy-free (if using dairy-free yogurt)
Vegan (if using maple syrup and dairy-free yogurt)

# PEANUT BUTTER BANANA BLISS SMOOTHIE

Prep Time: 5 – 7 minutes
Yield: 1 bowl

## INGREDIENTS:

- 1 ripe banana, frozen
- 2 tablespoons peanut butter
- ½ cup of almond milk (or milk of choice)
- ¼ cup Greek yogurt (or dairy-free yogurt)
- Optional: 1 teaspoon of organic honey
- Toppings: sliced banana, dark chocolate chips, mixed nuts

## STEPS:

**Prep & Blend**: Peel the ripe banana and break into pieces before freezing. Or grab the frozen bites you already have. Measure out the almond milk and the Greek yogurt. Have your peanut butter ready to mix. In a blender, add the banana, peanut butter, almond milk, Greek yogurt, and honey. Blend it up!

**Taste & Serve**: If you want it sweeter, add some organic honey. The consistency should be fine if using the frozen banana, but if you used a fresh banana, add some ice. Pour the peanut butter banana mixture into your favorite bowl and get ready to add toppings!

## TOPPING TIME!

- Sliced banana: for an extra fruity touch.
- Dark chocolate chips: for a delicious chocolatey surprise.
- A sprinkle of mixed nuts: (such as almonds, walnuts, or pecans) for a crunchy texture.

## NUTRITIONAL NOTES!

**Nutrient Boost**: Bananas offer natural sweetness and potassium for muscles and energy. Peanut butter adds healthy fats and protein for a satisfying treat. Greek yogurt provides creaminess and probiotics, while mixed nuts add protein, healthy fats, and fiber for a filling snack.

Gluten-free
Dairy-free (if using dairy-free yogurt)
Vegan (if using plant-based yogurt and skipping honey)

# BLUEBERRY YOGURT DELIGHT SMOOTHIE BOWL

Prep Time: 5 – 7 minutes
Yield: 1 bowl

## INGREDIENTS:

- 1 cup fresh or frozen blueberries
- ½ cup of almond milk (or milk of choice)
- ¼ cup Greek yogurt (or dairy-free yogurt)
- 1 tablespoon honey or maple syrup (optional)

- Optional: one teaspoon of organic honey or pure maple syrup
- Toppings: blueberries, granola, shredded coconut

## STEPS:

**Prep & Blend**: If using fresh blueberries, rinse under cold water. If using frozen, make sure they're ready to blend. Get the almond milk and Greek yogurt ready. In a blender, add the blueberries, almond milk, Greek yogurt, and honey or maple syrup. Blend until smooth and creamy. If you want a thicker consistency, add a bit more yogurt.

**Taste & Serve**: If you want it sweeter, add more honey or maple syrup. Pour the blueberry mixture into your favorite bowl and prepare for toppings!

## TOPPING TIME!

- Additional fresh blueberries: for a burst of flavor.
- A sprinkle of granola: for crunch.
- Shredded coconut: for a tropical twist.

## NUTRITIONAL NOTES!

**Nutritional Boost**: Blueberries offer antioxidants for heart and brain health, Greek yogurt adds probiotics for digestion, honey or maple syrup provides natural sweetness, and granola adds fiber and healthy fats for a satisfying crunch.

Gluten-free (if using gluten-free granola)
Dairy-free (if using dairy-free yogurt)
Vegan (if using plant-based yogurt and skipping honey)

# MANGO OAT PARADISE BOWL

**Prep Time:** 7-10 minutes
**Yield:** 1 bowl

## INGREDIENTS:

- 1 cup mango chunks (fresh or frozen)
- ¼ cup oats
- ¼ cup Greek yogurt (or dairy-free yogurt)
- ½ cup of almond milk (or milk of choice)
- Optional: one teaspoon of organic honey or pure maple syrup
- Toppings: mango slices, granola, chopped almonds and cashews

## STEPS:

**Prep & Blend**: With an adult's help, peel and chop fresh mango or use frozen. Soak oats in almond milk for 10 minutes to soften them. Measure your liquids, then blend mango, oats, Greek yogurt, and almond milk until smooth and creamy.

**Taste & Serve**: If you want it sweeter, add some honey or maple syrup. Pour the mango-oat mixture into your favorite bowl and get ready for topping!

## TOPPING TIME!

- Sliced fresh mango: for an extra fruity touch.
- A sprinkle of granola: for crunch.
- Chopped almonds and cashews: for added texture and healthy fats.

## NUTRITIONAL NOTES!

Mangoes provide vitamins A and C for skin and immunity, oats add fiber for digestion, Greek yogurt offers probiotics, and almonds and cashews give healthy fats and protein for a satisfying bowl.

Gluten-free (if using gluten-free oats and granola)
Dairy-free (if using dairy-free yogurt)
Vegan (if using plant-based yogurt and skipping honey)

# CHAPTER 4

# BONUS RECIPES! LET'S GET CREATIVE

# BONUS RECIPES!

Who says smoothies are only for sipping? In this chapter, we're taking smoothies to the next level with some super fun and creative recipes that you will love! From smoothie ice cream to slushies, these treats are perfect for warm days or when you want to shake things up. Whether you're making frozen smoothie pops or smoothie sandwiches, each recipe adds a playful twist to your favorite blends.

Get ready to explore new ways to enjoy your smoothies with these cool, tasty, and easy-to-make ideas.

# SMOOTHIE POPSICLES

Prep Time: 10 minutes
(+ 4-6 hours freezing time)
Yield: 6 smoothie pops

## INGREDIENTS:

- 1 cup mixed berries (strawberries, blueberries, raspberries)
- 1 ripe banana
- ½ cup Greek yogurt (or dairy-free yogurt)
- ½ cup of almond milk (or milk of choice)
- Optional sweetener: 1 tbsp of organic honey

**EXTRA MATERIALS NEEDED:** Popsicle molds and Popsicle sticks

## STEPS:

**Prep & Blend**: Wash the berries, peel the banana, and break it into little chunks. Measure out the yogurt and almond milk. In a blender, add the berries, banana, yogurt, almond milk, and honey/maple syrup. Blend until smooth and creamy.

**Fill the Molds**: Carefully pour the smoothie mixture into the popsicle molds, leaving a little room at the top for expansion during freezing.

**Insert Popsicle Sticks**: Once filled, insert the popsicle sticks into the molds. Make sure they are centered.

**Freeze**: Place the molds in the freezer for 4-6 hours or until the smoothie pops are fully frozen.

**Enjoy**: To release the smoothie pops from the mold, run the bottom of the molds under warm water for a few seconds. Then pull out your delicious smoothie pop and enjoy!

## NUTRITIONAL NOTES!

**Nutrient Boost**: Berries provide antioxidants and vitamin C for health, bananas add natural sweetness and potassium for energy, and yogurt offers protein for creaminess and fullness.

Gluten-free
Dairy-free (if using dairy-free yogurt)
Vegan (if using plant-based yogurt and skipping honey)

# CHOCOLATE SMOOTHIE ICE CREAM

**Prep Time:** 10 minutes (plus 3-4 hours of freezing time)
**Yield:** 4 servings

## INGREDIENTS:

- 2 ripe bananas
- 1 tablespoon unsweetened cocoa powder
- ½ cup yogurt (Greek or dairy-free)
- ½ cup of almond milk (or milk of choice)
- Optional sweetener: 1 tbsp of organic honey
- Optional: 1 teaspoon vanilla extract

**EXTRA MATERIALS NEEDED:** Freezer-safe container

## STEPS:

**Prep & Blend**: Peel and break bananas into chunks. Measure cocoa, yogurt, almond milk, and optional ingredients like honey or vanilla. Blend bananas, cocoa, yogurt, and almond milk until smooth. Add honey or syrup for extra sweetness, and blend again.

**Freeze the Mixture**: Pour the chocolate smoothie mixture into an ice cream mold or freezer-safe container. Smooth the top with a spoon and place it in the freezer for at least 3-4 hours until it's firm and ready to scoop.

**Scoop and Serve**: Once frozen, scoop the chocolate smoothie ice cream into bowls. For extra fun, sprinkle dark chocolate chips or a drizzle of peanut butter on top!

## NUTRITIONAL NOTES!

**Nutrient Boost**: Cocoa offers antioxidants and mood support, bananas add natural sweetness and potassium for energy, and yogurt provides protein and probiotics for a nutritious treat.

Gluten-free - Dairy-free (if using dairy-free yogurt) - Vegan (if using plant-based yogurt and skipping honey)

# SMOOTHIE SLUSHIES

**Prep Time:** 5 minutes
**Yield:** 2 servings

## INGREDIENTS:

- 1 cup frozen mango chunks
- ½ cup of orange juice (or any fruit juice of your choice)
- ½ cup ice cubes
- Optional sweetener: 1 tbsp of organic honey

## STEPS:

**Prep & Blend**: Measure out the frozen mango (or the fruit that you choose), orange juice, and ice cubes. If you're using honey or maple syrup, have it ready. Add the frozen mango, orange juice, and ice cubes to the blender. Blend on high until the mixture becomes slushy and smooth.

**Check the Consistency**: If your slushie is too thick, add a little more juice. If too thin, add a few more ice cubes.

**Serve the Slushies**: Pour the smoothie slushie into two large cups, pop in a straw, and enjoy your frosty treat!

## NUTRITIONAL NOTES!

**Tropical Boost**: Mangoes provide vitamin C and fiber for immune health, while orange juice adds sweetness, hydration, and extra vitamins.

Gluten-free - Dairy-free - Vegan (if using maple syrup)

# PEANUT BUTTER BANANA SMOOTHIE SANDWICHES

**Prep Time:** 10 minutes
**Yield:** 2 sandwiches

## INGREDIENTS:

- 1 ripe banana
- ½ cup Greek yogurt (or dairy-free yogurt)
- 3 tablespoons peanut butter (or almond butter)
- 4 healthy crackers (like whole-grain or seed-based)
- Optional sweetener: 1 tbsp of organic honey or pure maple syrup

**EXTRA MATERIALS NEEDED:** Spatula, Knife for spreading, Large plate

## STEPS:

**Prep & Blend**: Peel the banana, break into small chunks, and measure out the yogurt and peanut butter. Gather your healthy crackers and any optional sweeteners. In a blender, combine the banana, yogurt, peanut butter, and organic honey/maple syrup. Blend until smooth, thick, and creamy.

**Assemble the Sandwiches**: Spread the smoothie mixture generously on two crackers. Top with remaining crackers to create two sandwiches. You can add fresh banana slices for a tasty surprise. Bonus tip: pop your sandwiches in the freezer for ten minutes for a fresh snack!

**Slice and Serve**: If you like, you can break the sandwiches in half for easy handling. Arrange them on a plate for a pretty presentation.

## NUTRITIONAL NOTES!

**Nutrient Boost**: Bananas give sweetness, potassium, and energy, peanut butter adds healthy fats and protein, and Greek yogurt provides creaminess and probiotics for digestion.:

Gluten-free (if using gluten-free crackers) - Dairy-free (if using dairy-free yogurt) - Vegan (if using plant-based yogurt and skipping honey)

# SMOOTHIE ICE BITES

**Prep Time:** 10 minutes (plus freezing time)
**Yield:** About 24 ice cubes (depending on tray size)

## INGREDIENTS:

- 2 cups fruit smoothie (choose your favorite flavor from the previous chapters: strawberry, mango, or mixed berry)

- 1 cup fruit chunks (like diced strawberries, blueberries, or peaches)

**EXTRA MATERIAL NEEDED:** Ice cube trays, mixing bowl, spoon

## STEPS:

**Make the Smoothie**: Blend your favorite smoothie ingredients until smooth. For example, you can use frozen fruit, yogurt, and milk of choice to create a delicious and creamy base. Choose your favorite smoothie mix from Chapter 1.

**Mix in the Fun Additions**: In a mixing bowl, gently fold in the fruit chunks to the smoothie mixture. This adds texture and surprise bites to your ice cubes!

**Fill the Trays**: Pour the smoothie mixture into the ice cube trays. Fill them about three-quarters full to allow for expansion as they freeze.

**Freeze**: Place the trays in the freezer and let them freeze for at least 4-6 hours, or until completely solid.

**Serve and Enjoy**: Once frozen, remove the smoothie ice cubes from the trays. You can run warm water over the outside of the trays for a few seconds to help release them. Enjoy them on their own, drop them into drinks, or blend them into a quick smoothie later!

## NUTRITIONAL NOTES!

**Fruity Goodness**: These smoothie ice cubes are packed with the nutrients of fresh fruits and can be a fun way to enjoy vitamins and minerals in your drinks.

Gluten-free - Dairy-free (if using dairy-free yogurt and milk) - Vegan (if using plant-based yogurt and skipping honey)

# SMOOTHIE PANCAKE DRIZZLE

Prep Time: 5 minutes

Yield: About ½ cup (enough to drizzle over a stack of pancakes)

## INGREDIENTS:

- ½ cup mixed berries (strawberries, blueberries, or raspberries)
- ¼ cup Greek yogurt (or dairy-free yogurt)
- 2 tablespoons of almond milk (or milk of choice)
- Optional sweetener: 1 tbsp of organic honey or pure maple syrup
- Optional: 1 teaspoon vanilla extract

## STEPS:

**Prepare the Ingredients**: Wash the berries and measure out the yogurt, almond milk, and honey/maple syrup.

**Blend It Up**: In a blender, combine the berries, yogurt, almond milk, and vanilla extract. Blend until smooth. If it's too thick, add more almond milk until you get a drizzle consistency.

**Taste Test**: Give your drizzle a quick taste! If you want it sweeter, add some organic honey or maple syrup.

**Drizzle Away**: Pour the smoothie drizzle into a small jug or directly over your pancakes. You can also use it to top waffles, French toast, or even a bowl of oatmeal.

**Enjoy the Fruity Goodness**: Serve immediately over warm pancakes for a burst of fruity flavor with every bite.

## NUTRITIONAL NOTES!

**Berry Boost**: Berries offer antioxidants and vitamin C for immunity, yogurt adds creaminess, protein, and calcium, and honey or maple syrup keeps it low in processed sugars.

Gluten-free (as the drizzle is naturally gluten-free)
Dairy-free (if using dairy-free yogurt)
Vegan (if using plant-based yogurt and maple syrup)

# SMOOTHIE PARFAIT

**Prep Time:** 10 minutes
**Yield:** 1 parfait

## INGREDIENTS:

- 1 banana
- 1 cup plain or vanilla yogurt
- ¼ cup granola
- ¼ cup blueberries
- Optional sweetener: 1 tbsp of organic honey
- Optional: additional banana slices for topping

## STEPS:

**Blend**: In a blender, combine the banana, yogurt, and honey (if using). Blend until smooth and creamy.

**Layer**: In a glass or bowl, add a spoonful of granola at the bottom. Pour a layer of the banana smoothie on top.

**Add Fruit**: Add a few slices of banana and a handful of blueberries as the next layer.

**Repeat**: Repeat the layering process with more granola, smoothie, and fruit until you reach the top of your glass or bowl.

**Top It Off**: Finish with a sprinkle of granola, a few more banana slices, and blueberries for a colorful and crunchy topping.

## NUTRITIONAL NOTES!

**Nutrient Boost**: Bananas provide fiber and potassium for energy, while blueberries add antioxidants for cell protection.

Gluten-free (Use gluten-free granola to make this parfait suitable for those with gluten sensitivities)
Dairy-free (Swap the yogurt and milk with dairy-free alternatives like almond yogurt and coconut milk for a dairy-free option)
Nut-free (Make sure the granola is nut-free if there are any nut allergies)

# CONCLUSION

Congratulations on attempting this yummy and nutritious journey through the world of smoothies! Throughout this book, we've explored a bunch of recipes, from fruity blends bursting with flavor to vibrant veggie smoothies that are as surprisingly tasty as they are healthy. We've also dived into smoothie bowls that turn your favorite blends into visually stunning meals, and creative recipes that transform traditional smoothies into some pretty exciting treats.

The beauty of smoothies lies in their versatility. With countless combinations and the ability to cater to various dietary restrictions, there's something here for everyone. Whether you prefer dairy-free, Gluten-free, or Nut-free options, you can easily adapt these recipes to fit your needs while ensuring they remain wholesome and delicious.

Remember, smoothies are not just a quick fix for hunger; they can be a fun way to nourish your body and fuel your day. So, grab your blender, get creative, and enjoy the endless possibilities that smoothies offer for a healthier lifestyle. Cheers to your health and happiness—one smoothie at a time!

Made in the USA
Monee, IL
07 December 2024

72821590R00079